essential

Guide to Getting That Dream Job

Richard Winfield

Brefi Press
ThreeTicks.com

First published in 2024 by Brefi Press

ISBN 978-0-948537-43-1

www.threeticks.com

About the Author

Richard Winfield is the 'Independent Authority on Director Development'. A systems thinker with many years' experience as a management development consultant he specialises in director and board development, and corporate governance. He works internationally as a consultant, facilitator and trainer, providing away days, corporate retreats, workshops and board performance assessments; also coaching new directors and boards.

He has co-founded several companies and held non-executive directorship and board advisory roles.

Richard Winfield is highly qualified with a rich and varied career covering start-ups, privatisations and acquisitions with small, large and international organisations, public, private and third sector in the UK, Europe, USA, Middle East, Asia and Africa. A chameleon, he easily absorbs and relates to different cultures, whether they be organisational or geographical.

He has a master's degree in management, is a Master Practitioner of both NLP and Wealth Dynamics, and has been trained in leadership at the Disney Institute in Florida.

Richard is a past governor of the International Association of Coaching, who has published five books on coaching and created the definitive coaching course 'Invisible Coaching® - the art of natural coaching'.

He now focuses on director development and corporate governance, working internationally as a trainer and facilitator. He is the author of *The New Directors Handbook* and is the creator of the on-line ThreeTicks Academy, providing distance learning resources for director development. (www.threeticks.com)

Books by Richard Winfield

The New Directors Handbook

The AIM Directors Handbook

The NED Directors Handbook

Essential Checklists for Directors and Boards

Reflections of a Corporate Coach

Stories from a Corporate Coach

CPD Guides to:
Corporate Governance
Roles & Responsibilities of Directors
Becoming a Director
Networking as a Director
Building your own Support Network
Running Effective Meetings

Amazon.co.uk

Contents

Disclaimer: The author and publisher have used their best efforts in preparing this text and have drawn on a wide range of resources. The author and publisher do not provide legal advice and make no representation or warranties with respect to the accuracy, applicability, fitness, or completeness of this book. They shall not be liable for any loss or other damages, including but not limited to incidental, consequential of other damages.

1. What is the next step in your career?

Are you looking for a board level position?

If so, I can help you develop a compelling application that showcases your skills and experience and positions you as an exceptional candidate. I can prepare you for interviews and support you along your journey to success.

Securing a position at this level is a significant career milestone that requires careful planning and strategic actions.

The challenge

Obtaining a position as an executive or non-executive director is a significant milestone in any executive's career. However, these roles attract a large pool of highly qualified candidates, each with extensive experience and impressive credentials. It is a highly competitive market and success can take time.

Standing out in such a competitive environment requires more than just a stellar resume; it demands a unique value proposition and a strategic approach to self-promotion.

You will need a combination of education, experience, networking, and continuous self-improvement. Also a dedicated marketing strategy to get you onto shortlists.

The strategy

Networking plays a critical role in landing executive roles. Many C-suite and board positions are filled through referrals and connections rather than open job postings. Building a robust personal network of mentors, industry leaders and peers can offer support and recommendations.

A compelling **personal brand** that highlights your unique skills and achievements can set you apart from other candidates. This

1

involves more than just a polished Linkedin profile; it requires consistent effort to position yourself as a **thought leader** in your industry. Engaging in industry events, publishing articles, and maintaining an active presence on social media can enhance your visibility and reputation.

Soft skills such as leadership, communication and emotional intelligence are crucial for C-suite and board roles. Developing and demonstrating these skills is essential for success.

CVs, biographies and application letters comprise your formal job hunting package. They draw on your self-analysis, market analysis and job evaluation exercises and will benefit from excellent editorial, composition and design.

Interview skills and preparation: Having achieved your objective of joining a shortlist, your personal performance at the final selection stages will depend on meticulous preparation and coaching.

Due diligence

Not every opportunity will be right for you. Focus in areas that reflect your interests as well as your skills and experience; be prepared to look beyond the limits of your recent career. Due diligence before accepting a post should include cultural fit as well as understanding an organisation's mission, values, strategic goals and risk profile.

Developing relevant experience

Experience through smaller boards, advisory councils or non-profit organisations can provide valuable insights into governance and help you build a track record of success in board roles. Look out for such opportunities to enhance your record.

Where to start

The first step is for you to undertake a comprehensive appraisal of where you are now. Use the QR code overleaf to access our online assessment forms. These will provide excellent feedback on the steps needed to prepare you for your first application.

Even if you do not appear yet to have the profile for a typical board member, remember that you are unique and if you truly wish to make a contribution, there will be an organisation somewhere that needs what you have to offer. A structured development plan of training and experience will get you there.

How I can help you

I have a long and successful career as a consultant, coach and facilitator working internationally with individuals and teams at board level.

My natural talent for creative and logical thinking will bring structure and clarity to your thinking and help uncover transferable skills and experience you might not be aware of; then structure them to meet the needs of organisations you approach.

My experience as a publisher and author bring a wordsmithing and design ability to preparation of clear and powerful communication materials.

I look forward to working with you.

Richard Winfield
"The Independent Authority
on Director Development"

ThreeTicks.com/
assessments

3

2. Do you really want to become a director?

Do you really want to become a director? Ask yourself: why would anybody want to become a director?

A directorship role, whether as an executive or non-executive, is different from a management position.

Directorships bring risk, responsibility and no privileges!

Companies need directors to constitute a board and to direct their operations. But why would anyone choose to fulfil that role?

Let's get one thing straight first. Becoming a director has no relation with owning shares; you can be a director without owning shares, and you can own shares without becoming a director.

There are three elements in a company:

- the company itself
- the shareholders
- the directors

And these are entirely independent.

In addition there is a whole range of stakeholders to consider.

Health risk!

Limited liability applies to the company; it does not apply to the directors. It is important that you understand this and ensure that your board keeps proper records and follows proper processes and procedures.

Your biggest risk is likely to be financial. You must ensure that at all times the organisation can reasonably expect to be able to pay its creditors. The board must be constantly vigilant about wrongful trading, overtrading or trading fraudulently.

As a director you should at all times be able to demonstrate that the board has been exercising reasonable care, skill and diligence and that the directors have had regard to the likely consequences of any decision in the long term.

Directors can also be liable if the company fails to implement proper processes covering:

- Health and safety

- Employment law

- Control and disposal of hazardous waste

In the UK a director may also be liable for failure by the company to make required filings at Companies House.

You can mitigate these risks by taking out professional indemnity insurance and learning to become a professional and effective director.

Advisory board role

An alternative or intermediary role could be to join an advisory board. Properly constituted with appropriate terms of reference, this does not bring the same legal responsibilities as a formal directorship. Some business owners might welcome this as a first step towards sharing responsibility – but without giving away control – and it could be a useful means for you to gain experience.

The good news

Appointment as a director can be a natural stage in your career development and an exceedingly rewarding activity.

Directors are involved in an organisation at a higher, more strategic level. You would have greater leverage and can make a greater contribution.

It can also, of course, be financially rewarding; you should expect some compensation for your expertise, experience and the additional risk that you take on.

Here are some reasons for becoming a director quoted in the *Harvard Business Review*:

- Sitting on a board serves as an important signal, or "seal of approval" for an executive
- Board service is an avenue for an executive to gain access to unique knowledge, skills and connections
- Serving on a board increases an executive's likelihood of being promoted as a first-time CEO to an S&P 1500 firm by 44%
- Even if they aren't promoted, serving on a board boosts an executive's subsequent annual pay by 13%
- A board appointment is a strong signal that this leader has potential

"Ultimately board service is a key professional development tool in grooming potential CEOs that executives and boards alike are beginning to recognise and value."

3. Are you qualified to be a director?

There are two considerations before you should join a board.

Eligibility

Firstly, it is as well to be aware of any restrictions on you becoming a director:

- In the UK you must be over 16 years old
- You cannot also be the company's auditor
- You must not be an undischarged bankrupt
- You must not be disqualified from being a director by a court order

In addition, there might be relevant government regulations or restrictions in the company's Articles of Association that disqualify you from being a director of this particular company.

Time

Next, you should seriously consider the time commitment; do you have enough time and energy to serve as a director? How often does the board meet? Would you be required, maybe later, to take on more responsibilities, such as joining a committee or working party?

For you to be effective, you must be prepared to study board papers and find linkages and inconsistencies. You might need to follow up and clarify some of the information, or do some external research as part of your preparation.

You should allow time for away days, corporate retreats, study visits, social events, travel, reading and preparation for meetings.

In addition, you must be prepared to handle board emergencies, which come up at short notice and require intensive periods of full-time work and focus.

As a guide, you should reckon on 3-5 hours for each meeting and then allow three times that time for preparation; for a director of a large company this could amount to 300 hours a year.

Personal factors

In addition, you should consider your own suitability.

Here is a list of personal qualities that are important for directors:

- An effective and persuasive communicator whose contribution is concise, objective and clear.
- Socially competent with a deft touch of humour.
- Independent of mind without prejudicing loyalty to colleagues and the board.
- A good listener who can focus on key issues and respond with sound advice.
- Democratic in balancing the interests of shareholders against the interests of others involved in the business.
- An achiever in his or her own particular chosen field.
- Constructive in expressing ideas as an individual when divorced from the structure and props of his or her own organisation (non-executive directors)
- Positive in making statements and proposals, and unwilling to acquiesce in silence.

Here is a list of job-related competencies to consider:

- Strategic expertise – the ability to review the strategy through constructive questioning and suggestion.
- Accounting and finance – the ability to read and comprehend the company's accounts, financial material presented to the board, financial reporting requirements and some understanding of corporate finance.
- Financial and market awareness – the ability to recognise warning signs that might indicate a change in the overall health of the organisation.

- Legal – the board's responsibility involves overseeing compliance with numerous laws as well as understanding an individual director's legal duties and responsibilities.
- Managing risk – experience in managing areas of major risk to the organisation.
- Managing people and achieving change.
- Experience with financial markets.
- Industry knowledge – experience in similar organisations or industries.

You won't need to have all these yourself, but it is useful to identify your strengths. If there are any essential skills that you need, then you should either take steps to study them for yourself or attend a course – or you can negotiate coaching or training as part of your induction.

If you can identify gaps in a board's competence mix that you can fill, it could reinforce your application to join.

4. How to become a director

There are several routes to becoming a director depending on where you start from and your aspirations.

If you are a successful executive in a large company and are looking to become a director, then a worthwhile approach could be to gain experience as a director in a smaller company – a subsidiary of your group, or an independent company. In this case it would be useful to discuss your aspirations with your line manager and the human resources department, with particular consideration of conflict of interest.

Alternatively, there might be a traditional route of promotion to a board appointment within your current organisation.

Most likely, you will be looking for a non-executive directorship or advisory role. Good governance requires companies to have independent non-executive directors and there are recruitment organisations constantly looking for candidates.

Don't settle for joining any board, just for the experience – or worse still for the status.

Make a plan

Just the same as any project, you need an objective, a strategy and a plan.

What do you want? What size and age of company? Would you prefer established or entrepreneurial; service, manufacturing or professional services; public sector, private sector, or not-for-profit; local or international?

What have you got to offer? Have you got a specialist expertise, experience, or contacts? Are you a great team worker, or a master of detail? Have you been through a flotation, merger, acquisition, sale – or even a liquidation?

Do you have experience in turnarounds, growth or change programmes?

Somewhere there will be an organisation facing a similar situation in the future, but lacking experience that you already have.

Where are you now? Take a serious look at your CV. Make a note of everything that you have achieved, the challenges that you have faced. Build up your personal inventory.

Finally, of course . . .

What do you want to achieve? As you conduct this analysis it is likely that you will start to refine your ideas about what you would like to achieve. What would be a reasonable first appointment? Do you need breadth of experience or depth? What areas would you most like to be involved in? What sort of people would you like to work with?

The more accurately you can describe the perfect situation, the more effectively you can develop a successful strategy and describe what you are looking for to others, and the greater the likelihood that you will notice opportunities as they arise.

Fine tune your reticular activating system (look it up) and you will be surprised what you see.

Get professional support. However rigorous your self-analysis, you will benefit from the support of a third party with assessment tools, an analytical mind and a proven model of success.

Build a track record. The earlier you can start, the better; even at school or university, committee experience provides a grounding. However, you are probably much more advanced in your career; but it is never too late.

You could research the opportunity of joining a voluntary organisation, either business-related or social. This could range from a sports club or charity to joining an education or hospital trust. Apart from gaining experience, you are likely to meet other professionals who could be useful additions to your network.

The more, and earlier, the experience you can get, the better. BUT. Know what you want, and avoid accepting the first opportunity that arises; it might appear attractive now but could prevent you from taking a better opportunity later.

5. Building a strategy for success

Personal inventory

Your first step should be to ask "Where am I now?" Your next role will be a foundation for your future career, so it is worth considering the wider context:

- Are you introvert or extrovert, do you like challenge, travel?
- What are your personal values; what is important to you, have you thought about your legacy?
- What do you really enjoy? What do you not enjoy?
- What types of people, organisations do you wish to work with?
- Do you enjoy challenge, risk, variety – or a more stable environment?
- Where do you live and how much time have you got to offer?
- What is your present role, position, status, reputation at your current employer? How strong is it? How well known is it?
- What family and social support can you call on? Are there likely to be any conflicts of interest in time, energy, or relationships? How much support/understanding can you rely on?
- Have you got a mentor – or mentors – who can help you?

Discover your strengths and talents

I once heard a speaker ask "What is talent?" Answer: "Easy to learn and easy to do!" The consequence is that you are less likely to value your strengths and talents than things you had to work hard to learn. This means you need a rigorous process for identifying them.

There are plenty of psychometric systems available and you'll find reference to our self-assessment forms in the appendix.

If possible some form of 360° feedback can be very helpful – even just asking colleagues, preferably with scoreable questionnaires so they are not tempted to be polite!

You may be surprised at what you find in your own history – skills and experiences that you have forgotten, or devalued.

Review your connections

Your network can be one of your most valuable assets. Most people will be happy to help with suggestions and advice.

Remember the adage "It is not who you know, it is who they know." Your personal contacts can be useful, but your contacts' contacts might be even more useful. However, for them to help you they need to have a clear and memorable understanding of exactly what you are looking for.

First thing that you can do is to review your professional relationships. LinkedIn is there for that purpose, but you will surely have lots of informal contacts in your database, people who know you or have done business with you.

And don't ignore 'social' social media like Facebook; people who know you personally and whose own networks might be relevant.

Organisations like BNI, breakfast clubs, professional organisations work on this basis. However, make sure you choose communities consistent with the people you need to meet. It is too easy to waste time eating breakfasts with 'butchers, bakers and candlestick makers'. Be selective.

Social media

Social media gives you not only an opportunity to extend your connections, but also a searchable database, a publishing channel and a learning forum. LinkedIn should be considered essential.

Remember to apply the same ethical standards and courtesies you would expect elsewhere.

Improve your networking skills

Networking is not about selling. It is about building a network of people you 'know, like and trust'. It takes time. There is a different quality of relationship the second time you meet someone from the first time. It is often said that it takes seven touches to make a sale, perhaps it takes seven contacts to build a relationship. These need not all be the same. The more often you connect in different contexts, the more powerful the reinforcement; publishing and social media included.

Denver-based board advisor Tracy Houston recommends an active approach. Have a clear board-level value proposition, know who you need to meet with based on your directorship strategy, attend networking events to meet these targeted contacts in person, join associations where these people hold memberships, and speak at executive level events hosted by the industry you have targeted in your strategy to gain a board seat.

Networking is about listening, so bring your curiosity. Where possible, endeavour to assist others, particularly by introducing or recommending others. Remember to follow up – and make a Linkedin connection. Always carry an appropriate business card – and make use of the back of the card for a message or more information.

Optimise your public and media profile

If you want to be found, you need to stand out; also it helps if the right people know what you are looking for.

Your public profile has both a sales function and a qualification role. A powerful profile will get you noticed and establish your authority and competence. You can be sure that recruiters will use Linkedin to find you and to check out your claims.

Put yourself about: write articles, join Internet forums and contribute to discussions, write a blog, put videos on YouTube, attend conferences, networking groups, turn up at annual general meetings (you might end up on a committee).

You could also write a book, or two! The technology is free, digital printing means no upfront investment, Amazon will handle the sales and short books (like this one) are increasingly acceptable. And in your book – include the perfect sales pitch *i.e.* your bio!

There is a great deal of kudos in being a published author; it proves that you have taken the trouble to master and explain a subject. You can slip a copy into any correspondence and leave one as a gift when you first meet a valuable contact. It beats a business card any day.

Ensure your profile is complete, highlighting your key achievements, skills, and experiences that align with board-level positions. Regularly share thought leadership content related to your industry to demonstrate your expertise and insights. Engage with relevant posts and groups to increase your visibility and network with other professionals. Remember that ALL social media activity is relevant, so behave ethically and consider the pros and cons of any controversial comments.

Additionally, you can leverage traditional media to build your credibility and reach a broader audience. Contribute to industry publications, speak at conferences, and participate in panels. By consistently presenting yourself as a knowledgeable and influential figure in your field, you enhance your reputation and make yourself an attractive candidate.

Develop an effective marketing package

You should create a comprehensive marketing package to clearly articulate your value proposition, showcase your achievements, and demonstrate your readiness for top executive positions.

This will include a professional biography, executive resume/CV, personal branding statement, cover letter, portfolio of case studies and presentations, and recommendations and testimonials from colleagues and clients who have agreed to be contacted.

Ensure that you have template documents in both digital and hard copy formats that can be rapidly amended to suit the requirements of target posts. You might also consider a video introduction that highlights your career journey, leadership style, what you are looking for and what you have to offer. Make sure it is to an acceptable professional quality.

Preparation

For each application you'll need to research the organisation and study the leadership. Search for any recent media coverage with particular interest in anything controversial.

Similarly for the industry, looking for developments in regulations, technology and the market.

Enquire about the selection process, timing, number of stages, who will interview you. They might be prepared for you to visit premises or meet staff as part of your preparation.

Interviews

Once you have been selected for a shortlist, you will need to shine at one or more interviews.

The secret sauce of interview preparation is for you to become the interviewer. You need to do your research. A powerful way to prepare for an interview is swap roles. Instead of preparing as an applicant, play the role of the interviewing panel. Get into their minds, find out what they are looking for. You will then be able to generate some challenging questions they might ask.

You might discover, for example, that they doubt your eligibility for the role, especially if you are from a different business sector. In which case you might need to coach them on why they should expand their thinking.

You will be in a stronger position to answer any questions they might ask – and to control the conversation. Role play the interview; ideally ask someone to ask the questions you have devised.

Improving your interview skills

Polish Your Communication Skills

- **Clear and Concise**: Practice speaking clearly and concisely. Avoid jargon and focus on communicating your points effectively.

- **Confident and Personable**: Exude confidence without arrogance. Show your personality and build rapport with the interviewers.

Prepare for Case Studies and Presentations

- **Case Study Preparation**: Some interviews include a case study, so practice analysing data, developing strategies, and presenting your solutions.

- **Presentation Skills**: Be ready to deliver a polished and persuasive presentation. Focus on clear visuals and articulate delivery.

Simulate the Interview Environment

- **Mock Interviews**: Conduct mock interviews with a mentor or career coach. Simulate the interview environment to build confidence and receive feedback.

- **Technical Setup**: If the interview is virtual, ensure your technology is reliable. Check your internet connection, camera, and microphone ahead of time.

Preparing for the interview

Clarify Your Value Proposition

- What would be the unique value you bring to the table? Focus on how your skills, experience and vision align with the company's goals.

- Identify some specific achievements and how they could translate to success in the role you are applying for. Use quantifiable metrics to highlight your impact.

Prepare for common and challenging questions

- **Standard Questions**: Rehearse answers to common executive-level questions about your leadership style, conflict resolution, and strategic planning.

- **Behavioural Questions**: Use the STAR method (Situation, Task, Action, Result) to prepare for behavioural questions that require you to discuss past experiences.

- **Thought Leadership**: Be ready to share your thoughts on industry trends, future challenges, and innovative solutions. Demonstrating your foresight and strategic thinking is crucial.

Develop Insightful Questions

- **Show Engagement**: Prepare questions that demonstrate your deep understanding of the company and your interest in its future. Ask about company culture, strategic priorities, and key challenges.

- **Strategic Inquiries**: Pose questions that reflect your strategic thinking, such as inquiries about long-term goals, market opportunities, and risk management.

Craft Your Narrative

- **Tell Your Story**: Be prepared to tell a compelling narrative of your career journey. Highlight the pivotal moments, key decisions, and lessons learned.

- **Growth Attitude**: Demonstrate a willingness to learn and adapt. Highlight how you have grown from past experiences and how you plan to continue evolving.

- **Vision for the Future**: Discuss your vision for the role and how you plan to contribute to the company's growth and success.

Attending the interview

Remember, the interview should be a two-way conversation; your participation will influence their questions, your engagement will demonstrate your competence and both parties should recognise that, although they have to decide whether to make you an offer, you are also there to decide whether to accept it.

Positive Mindset: Approach each interview with a positive and proactive mindset. Visualise success and manage stress through relaxation techniques.

Arrive Early: Aim to arrive at least 15 minutes early to account for any unforeseen delays and to demonstrate punctuality.

Dress Appropriately: Dress in a manner that is appropriate for the company's culture. Typically, formal business attire is expected for executive roles. Ensure you are well-groomed. First impressions are critical, and a polished appearance conveys professionalism.

Bring Necessary Documents: Bring several copies of your resume and supporting documents, neatly organised in a portfolio. Include references, certificates, and any other documents that may support your candidacy.

Body Language: Sit up straight, maintain good eye contact, and offer a firm handshake. Nod and show attentiveness when the interviewer is speaking. Avoid crossing your arms or appearing uninterested.

Communicate Clearly and Concisely: Answer questions clearly and directly. Avoid rambling; instead, structure your responses using the STAR method (Situation, Task, Action, Result) when appropriate. Maintain a positive tone throughout the interview. Highlight your achievements and how they can benefit the company.

6. Checks to make before accepting any directorship

What to do when you get an offer

Don't accept it! Seriously, do your due diligence and research the organisation. Consider the opportunity cost as well as the opportunity.

Do culture and relationships fit?

Organisations can have a wide range of cultures – their unspoken norms of behaviour – that are critical to a company's success. Some see themselves as competitive, with a sporting analogy, some are more military in their approach. Others are creative, or cutting edge. Some are nurturing a new entity or are stewards for a legacy.

The culture and your potential contribution are likely to be different according to whether this is a young or mature company, whether it is growing or in distress, it is private or public, or preparing for a flotation, merger or acquisition.

Organisation culture is a powerful force that reflects and shapes the way an organisation operates. It is part of why people work there and even why people do business with it.

Board culture

Creating business value is the job of the board – in which no-one holds individual formal power. That's very different from the hierarchy of corporate management and you should consider how you will prepare yourself for this.

Before deciding to join a particular board you should carry out your own exercise of due diligence. If you are not comfortable with an organisation's culture, you are unlikely to give of your best, or to want to stay for a full term.

One of the most important subjects to consider is the judgement, experience and temperament of the board and senior management, and whether you will enjoy working with them.

Speaking with directors or management on a one-on-one basis will help you appreciate this. You might be able to contact directors or senior management who have recently left the company. If so, what were the circumstances of those departures? Do they reveal anything about the dynamic between the board and management?

Starting at a basic level, you will need an insight into the experience and background of the directors and senior management.

Does the CEO encourage open and collaborative environments between the board and management? Is the CEO committed to listening to the board's input, and can directors interact with senior management without the presence of the Chief Executive?

It is worth committing significant time and resources to finding out everything you can before taking up a position.

Meeting the directors

You can start with your conversation with the chairman and by meeting as many of the current directors as possible. You should also ask for and read the last two years' worth of board minutes. These will give you an excellent insight into both the culture and the processes.

Here are some of the questions you should ask yourself:

- What are the other directors like? Do you share their values and aspirations for the company?
- How capable and committed are they? Do they appear qualified for their roles?
- Who are the current chief executive and non-executive directors, what is their background and record and how long have they served on the board?

- Are they people of integrity, willing to ask difficult questions and are they there to make a contribution – or flatter their egos?
- How do they operate as a board? Do a few dominant directors commandeer the meeting? Are there factions? Does superficial knowledge go unchallenged? Is the chemistry collaborative?
- What is the size and structure of the board and board committees and what are the relationships between the chairman and the board, the chief executive and the management team?
- Are there directors who dominate board deliberations or who discourage meaningful discussion or dissent?
- Are there directors who serve as an effective counterbalance to management?
- Does the board have good processes? Are discussions relevant, rigorous and penetrating? Is the board equipped to handle corporate life-threatening issues?
- Do directors think, question and challenge, or are board meetings ritualistic, with tick box governance, inadequate understanding and a focus on short term and internal issues?
- How do they deal with challenge, risk and conflict? Do they demonstrate curiosity to question and courage to challenge? Are they alert to risks and the reality of what is happening around them; do they think for themselves?

When you have answered these you will be in a position to decide whether you have a good fit with the board, directors and management, and whether you will be able to add real value.

Check governance

Corporate governance is about what the board of a company does and how it sets the values of the company. It is to be distinguished from the day-to-day operational management of the company by full-time executives. It is important for non-executive directors to recognise this; executive directors must learn to wear two hats.

Good governance is not just about compliance with formal rules and regulations. It is about establishing internal processes and attitudes that add value, enhance the reputation of the business, make it more attractive to external investors and lenders and ensure its long-term success.

Poor corporate governance weakens the company's potential and at worst can pave the way for financial difficulties and even fraud.

What is this board's approach?

When considering whether to join a board, you should determine whether it takes a positive approach to its fiduciary and compliance duties and has formal structures that ensure that key issues are addressed in advance.

Or is it a passive board that approaches governance as a box-ticking exercise?

Good governance requires that the performance of the board be evaluated once a year. Well conducted evaluations help the board, committees and individual directors perform to their maximum capabilities.

So a good start would be to ask what steps the board takes to evaluate its performance and that of its committees and individual directors – and to obtain a copy of the latest report.

Process checklist

Here are some questions you should ask yourself:

- Is the company committed to compliance?
- What record does the company have on corporate governance issues?
- Does the company have sound and effective systems of internal controls?

- What are the processes for setting the agenda, board meetings and minutes?
- How does the board address decision-making, strategy and monitoring of performance?
- Does the board have off-site residential retreats or away days?
- How does the board differentiate between board responsibilities and management roles?
- Does the board have an effective committee structure?
- Does the board have a formal process for dealing with complaints and whistle blowers?
- Who owns the company; who are the main shareholders and how has the profile changed over recent years?
- What is the company's attitude towards, and relationship with, its shareholders?

Answering these questions will enable you to decide how well organised and structured the board is, whether the directors aspire to best practice and whether it is aligned with your values.

Check out the financial health

You do not need to be an expert in accounting but you must be satisfied that any board you join has the necessary expertise both on the board and available to you.

You also need to check that is has robust processes in place and that information is monitored and reported on a regular basis.

Before joining a board you should check out its financial health.

- What is the company's current financial position and what has its financial track record been over the last three years?
- What are the exact nature and extent of the company's business activities?

- What is the company's competitive position and market share in its main business areas?
- What are the key dependencies (e.g. regulatory approvals, key licences)?
- Does it have sufficient reserves?
- Is its projected cash flow adequate?
- How does cash flow vary through its business cycle/through the month?
- How does the board monitor financial performance against budget?
- What checks and balances are in place to detect errors, fraud and abuse?
- Are any specific expense areas rising faster than sources of income?

As a director you will potentially be at risk if things go wrong. Are you satisfied that this company is soundly financed, has adequate systems and a responsible approach?

It might be that you are looking for the challenge of a turnaround. In which case it is even more important that you are aware of what risks you might be taking on.

Risk and risk appetite

Successful business involves taking risks.

As a member of a board should have a feeling for the main business risks and you should ensure there are ways of monitoring these risks. Boards should have nominated directors with risk expertise and every company should approve the risk appetite framework, including internal control reporting and independent, coordinated, assurance over controls that mitigate each risk and their interactions.

Risk assessment and control should not be limited to financial risks but should also take account of an increasing range of factors such as employment litigation, loss of key individuals, succession planning, IT failure/data loss, reputation risk etc.

Rapid technology advancement has created further opportunity and risk. Cyber security, employees using their own computers and mobile devices, and social media are just three IT risks that now need internal controls to avoid privacy breaches, reputational damage and significant investor loss.

Similar risks apply for corporate manslaughter and, potentially, for environmental damage. In many countries there is additional risk from accusations of bribery, modern slavery and human trafficking. You must be satisfied that the board has implemented and monitors appropriate processes and training of employees and suppliers in each of these areas.

Regulators are now able to hold boards responsible for fraud, bribery and other forms of corruption at deep level within and even interacting outside the organisation. They are imposing onerous risk coverage requirements on directors that require oversight of internal controls, risk-takers and limitations.

In smaller companies directors are sometimes asked to guarantee loans to the company. Make sure you are aware of any such obligations as you would be put at risk if the loan conditions are not fulfilled.

Risk profile

Before joining a board you should ensure that you understand the type and level of risk and that it is compatible with your own risk appetite.

A good start would be to ask to see the company's risk register. Check not only what is in it, but judge how comprehensive it is and ask how regularly it is reviewed.

- Does the board commission independent reviews of the board, risks and internal controls to provide it with advance warning on precisely where their vulnerabilities and weaknesses are?

- Has the company implemented confidential whistle-blowing and amnesty procedures, and audits of internal controls over culture and reputation?
- Is there anything about the company's business activities that would cause you concern in terms of risk and any personal ethical considerations?
- Is any material litigation, investigation or other claim presently being undertaken or threatened, either by the company or against it?
- Are you satisfied that the internal regulation of the company is sound and that you would be able to operate within its governance framework?
- What insurance cover is available to directors and what is the company's policy on indemnifying directors?

Conflicts of interest

In a company you may have several roles – as well as acting as a director, you might also own shares, lend the company money and guarantee loans, be a supplier or customer, or other significant stakeholder. Conflicts of interest bring a further level of risk.

If you become a director of more than one company you should pay particular attention to the potential for conflicts of interest. You must not divert business opportunities to yourself or to others that ought to be available to the whole company, nor should you benefit from a third party by reason of your being a director, or by doing or not doing something.

Board purpose

Does this company have a meaningful mission?

If you are to remain motivated, it is important to have a good reason for joining any particular board.

Would working for this company be worthwhile in its own right, or are you attracted by challenges it is facing or, perhaps, by the status associated with being on its board?

Although the primary task for all boards is to establish corporate direction, this is often the area in which boards find it most difficult to spend sufficient time and about which directors most frequently report the inadequacy of their knowledge.

A purpose you can relate to combined with a good cultural fit would be a good indicator that this is a project you can commit to, potentially for two terms of three years.

Company mission

A shared understanding of a company's purpose and long term vision is important because it provides the context for strategy and decision making.

Here are some factors to consider:

- Does the company have a defined vision, mission and values statement?
- Does this:
    - o give a sense of the future
    - o guide decision making and strategy
    - o create a shared purpose
    - o provide guidelines that determine behaviour
    - o inspire emotion
    - o connect to values
- Are the annual report and corporate strategy consistent with the organisation's defined purpose?
- Does the board hold regular off-site retreats or away days to review its purpose and consider strategy?
- Are its plans consistent with the corporate strategy
- Are plans compatible across different business units

o Individual and combined plans are achievable within the resources available, and the forecast revenues and costs

o Plans are consistent with and potentially responsive to changes in market, economy and regulatory environments

o Plans are consistent with legal and ethical requirements

o Plans are supported by the management

Personal role

If you identify with the company's purpose then it is worth exploring exactly what your role will be. Why have you been invited to join the board?

If you are an executive director your role and status will probably be connected to your role as a head of department or functional expert. Nevertheless, you should discuss with the chairman exactly what he or she expects of you.

If you are an external appointment to a non-executive role, there are more issues for you to clarify.

Here are some reasons why you might have been approached:

- To provide instant management or functional experience
- To add prestige or respectability to the board
- To bring experience of proposed activities such as a flotation, merger or takeover
- To strengthen defences against possible takeover approaches or shareholder activity
- To bring your influence and access to your network of contacts
- As a potential successor to the chairman
- To support the chairman's power base
- To represent a dominant shareholder
- As part of a board shake-up following new ownership, new chairman or an internal upheaval

- To replace a retiring director
- To create a better balance of experience, respond to a changing business environment
- To rejuvenate a tired or aging board
- To support diversity policies

Discussing these with the chairman will not only clarify what is expected you, but it might also enable you to highlight additional talents. Alternatively, it might identify warning signals.

7. Shortlist and Shine

How to get onto shortlists and stand out at interviews

What I can do for you

This is not a CV writing service. With my critical and structured thinking, knowledge of corporate governance combined with design and wordsmithing skills from my publishing background, I can help you truly understand your potential, and create the promotional materials that get you onto shortlists.

As an experienced corporate coach with international experience working at board level, I can help you develop confidence, improve your networking performance and prepare for interviews.

Obtaining a top level position is the same as any other business project. You need a strategy, a plan and preparation. I can help you with these.

The first step is to build a powerful personal brand. I offer a proven process that starts with a comprehensive investigation of your values, knowledge, experience and public profile, identifying your unique talents and reassessing your career goals. Then to identify the types of roles and organisations that attract you – often outside your current business or industry.

Lay the foundation

Create a compelling Linkedin Profile: Linkedin plays an important role in recruitment. Recruiters use it to trawl for candidates and then to satisfy themselves that you fulfil their needs. It is an essential sales document.

CV/Resume: This is a necessary information document to get you past the HR gatekeepers. It should be comprehensive and support your application.

Build your personal brand: Position yourself as an expert in your field by publishing articles, speaking at events and being active on social media.

Expand your network: Decide who you should meet, join professional organisations, attend industry conferences and engage in networking events to build and strengthen your professional connections.

Personal Development Plan: The process above is likely to identify soft skills you need to improve, as well as professional/technical gaps.

Template application letters: Each application should be carefully researched and a bespoke covering letter composed. However, a pre-prepared template in your own style that can be adapted for individual applications will save time and ensure all essential matters are covered.

Respond to an opportunity

When you become aware of an opportunity we then prepare a formal application.

Research the organisation: Learn what we can to prepare the application and decide whether to proceed.

Prepare specific documents: Take advantage of the work done above to customise documents for the formal application. Some will be needed to fulfil the system requirements, others as your sales message.

Invitation to interview: This is where we draw on my coaching skills to prepare you emotionally and to work through the spectrum of questions and answers.

How I work with clients

When you're aiming for top-level success, especially in a non-executive director role, having a wide range of experience is essential. My career is a testament to this. The diverse skills I've honed over the years come together to create the comprehensive package I offer you.

Innovation and Thought Leadership

At every stage of my career, I've been at the forefront of innovation and a thought leader. My journey has taken me through software development and application since the mainframe era, award-winning transportation planning, newspaper publishing and authorship, executive coaching, management consulting, facilitating, and training. I've collaborated with small private companies, the public sector, and multinational corporations. Now, I focus on director development and corporate governance.

The Power of Structure and Clarity

My natural talent lies in seeking structure and clarity, challenging accepted ideas, and systems. My motivation is to make sense of the world – and your world too. Read how I helped John, Ian and Sarah:

"Richard puts you at ease without you knowing it. I thought I was having a casual conversation but by the end I realised that he had identified an entirely new perspective of my skill set. That's the power of a good listener."

John Morris, Director
Public Affairs

"Richard's ability to bring structure and clarity to my strategic career decision-making and to focus on introspection has enabled me to bring a deep understanding of my strengths and experience. I commend him to you."

Ian Parry-Belcher
Project Manager

"I contacted Richard because I was dissatisfied with my current role. After two sessions on Zoom I decided that I would be happy to stay for a couple more years but, in the meantime, lay the foundation for a new role thereafter."

Sarah McDade
Programme
Manager

Document Preparation

Crafting a compelling narrative across different platforms is crucial for securing high-level roles. There are three specific documents that you must produce, each tailored to different styles and purposes:

LinkedIn Profile

Your LinkedIn profile is your professional online presence. It serves as a digital resume and networking tool, allowing you to connect with industry leaders, recruiters, and potential employers. It also showcases your skills, experiences, and accomplishments to a global audience.

We'll craft a headline that captures your personality and professional essence, and a summary that highlights your career achievements and goals. Detailed descriptions of your roles, skills endorsements, and recommendations from colleagues will bolster your profile's credibility. I'll ensure your profile is optimised with relevant keywords to increase visibility to recruiters.

CV (Curriculum Vitae)

The CV provides a comprehensive overview of your career. It should highlight your academic background, professional experience, skills, and achievements in detail.

We'll develop a structured and concise CV that includes a clear career objective or personal statement, a detailed work history with quantifiable achievements, education, certifications, and relevant skills. It will be tailored to emphasise the aspects of your career that align with your target roles, making it easier for recruiters and hiring managers to confirm your fit for the position.

Application Letter

The application letter (or cover letter) is your opportunity to make a personal connection with the hiring manager. It is your essential sales document. It introduces you, explains why you're interested in the role, and how your skills and experiences make you the ideal candidate. This letter is often the first impression you make, so it needs to be a compelling narrative that aligns with the job description, highlighting your most relevant experiences and achievements.

The letter will be personalised to reflect your genuine interest in the company and the specific role. It will include a strong opening, a concise body that aligns your qualifications with the job requirements, and a closing that reiterates your enthusiasm and calls for the next step in the hiring process.

By presenting a cohesive and compelling narrative across all platforms, we'll maximise your chances of standing out and securing your dream job.

Coaching for Interviews

Finally, we shall prepare for each interview. My goal is to equip you with the tools and strategies needed to successfully navigate any interview and secure your desired position. Personalised coaching with me will ensure you present your best self and effectively communicate your qualifications and vision. It will boost your confidence, refine your interview skills, and ensure you leave a lasting positive impression.

Conclusion

Follow these steps and you'll be equipped with a strategic roadmap to not only find but also secure your dream job. By working with me, you'll gain clarity, uncover hidden potential, and develop a strategic path to achieve your goals.

Let's work together to turn your aspirations into reality and pave the way for a successful and fulfilling career.

Appendix

I have created a series of online self-assessment forms to support you in your journey towards achieving that dream job. On completion, you will receive summary forms as the basis for discussion with a coach, and for plotting your progress.

Dream Job Readiness Assessment

The Dream Job Readiness assessment will help you determine your initial readiness and then plot your progress as you prepare to apply for that first job. Structured questions help you assess your readiness in each of these areas.

Strengths:

Discover and clarify your unique abilities, skills and achievements. Define the unique value you could bring to a new role, allowing you to highlight these strengths effectively in your application materials.

Connections:

Review the strength and relevance of your professional network. Make sure you are nurturing and maintaining existing connections and are actively involved in professional communities and social media.

Public Profile:

Evaluate the effectiveness of your public profile and personal branding. Review your LinkedIn profile to align with your career goals and make a positive impression on recruiters and interviewers.

Social Media:

Assess your proficiency in leveraging social media; review your engagement, thought leadership content, and online interactions to ensure they are appropriate to C-suite and board-level roles.

Networking Skills:
Evaluate your ability to build relationships with key industry professionals. Identify opportunities to expand your network and uncover new opportunities.

CV/Resume:
Review the strength and effectiveness of your CV/resume. Evaluate the clarity, relevance, and impact of your qualifications, accomplishments, and experience in terms of board-level positions.

Application Letters:
Craft persuasive application letters that communicate your fit for each position, align your qualifications with the organisation's needs, and articulate your passion and motivation for the role.

threeticks.com/
dream-job-readiness

Other useful assessment tools

Here are some more assessment tools to help you along your journey:

Evaluate Your Personal Effectiveness:

Take a basic audit of your self-awareness, self-development, assertiveness, communication, time management, problem solving, decision-making and use of social media.

Strategic Management:

Review your ability to evaluate and improve performance, set strategy, organise and delegate work, create a diverse and collaborative culture. Assess your ability to monitor the external environment.

Company Director:

Identify your personal qualities and effectiveness in terms of board level behaviour. Assess your understanding of governance, finance and strategy, and the need for further study.

threeticks.com/
assessments